The *Beauty* of PUBLIC EDUCATION

Ten Essentials

Ian Bruce Kelsey, Ph.D.

Published by the
Ian Bruce Kelsey Education Centre Ltd.
4070 West 37th Avenue,
Vancouver, British Columbia, Canada V6N 2W7
Phone/Fax: (604) 261-6441

Canadian Cataloguing in Publication Data

Kelsey, Ian Bruce, (date)
The beauty of public education

Includes index.
ISBN 0-9684610-0-X

1. Education. 2. Public Schools. I. Title.
LB14.7.K44 1999   370'.1   C98-911186-5

Typesetting and Jacket Design
by Westpoint Graphics, Vancouver
Printed and bound by Electric Print Ltd. Vancouver

Designed for the child
of the 21st Century
and beyond.

Contents

Preface

After years of travelling the pathways of education, I came to the conclusion that all education is character education, the unfoldment of innate qualities which enables learners to realize their potential.

I arrived at this conclusion through practical and not theoretical means, solely through experience, reason, and intuition. I discovered through my own travels that the paths of a sound education lead to the same destination: *freedom* – freedom from limitation and freedom to use talents and abilities without inhibition. That freedom dawns gradually. Individuals need time to work out their own destiny, and to realize they have an obligation to contribute to society. This uncovering of potential, often hidden or unknown, leads to self-government, to humility, to power. It leads to vitality and activity, with regenerative interludes of solitude and stillness. It leads to peace and goodwill, to unselfishness and responsibility, to a life of productivity and prosperity.

Character education is a process whereby students take part in school activities planned to produce the educated citizen. This citizen is a problem-solver, a producer, a doer, an independent thinker; someone who is thoughtful, respectful, cooperative, principled; someone who is flexible, imaginative, creative. Growth in these attributes occurs slowly as the student follows the direction and inspiration provided by teachers through the academics, athletics, arts, and other activities offered.

Prime responsibility for this growth rests with the student, and depends largely upon receptivity to the teaching provided. But that growth is enhanced by the quality of the teachers the individual has over many years. It is essential therefore that those teachers be of the highest calibre possible in terms of character, and that *all* who work in public schools be of a similar calibre.

It is the right of all children throughout the world to benefit from an education system that sets them free, and the system that does that best is public universal character education, because it brings together children from widely diverse backgrounds where they learn naturally to study, to work, and to play together. And that in time will help produce the peace and goodwill the world is always in need of.

Set forth in the following pages are the essential elements in that education, an education that makes for a healthy individual, a strong country, and a civilized society – free, progressive, diverse, and democratic. These elements were first published by the author in 1993 in a book titled *Universal Character Education*. The book has since been revised solely for clarity, conciseness, and clear identification of what the author believes are the ten essential elements of successful public education, ideas imperative for parents, politicians, and public school teachers.

CHAPTER 1

Philosophy

The responsibility of educating children belongs to parents. Before any statement of philosophy on public education is set forth, it needs to be clearly understood that the public schools belong to parents, not to the state nor to teachers, and that parents, through a board of governors, hire teachers to teach, to educate, to elevate their children.

There really is only one philosophy of education, only one statement of fundamental belief for the education of children and that is: all education is the unfoldment of character, with unfoldment occurring only through development of the whole person, including the moral, mental, emotional, social, physical, creative, and spiritual dimensions.

The spiritual refers to cultivation of a love of good in any form, with emphasis on love of one another; moral refers to an awareness of right and wrong and a willingness to act in accord with one's highest sense of right; mental refers to cultivation of things of the mind and an ability to think for oneself; emotional refers to the expression and control of feelings, sensitivity to the feelings of others and a consideration of those feelings; social refers to the ability and willingness to interact with others on a wholesome basis; physical refers to participation in vigorous physical activities; and creative refers to cultivation of an attitude that promotes fresh approaches to problems and their solutions.

Education is the same wherever it takes place. The same quality of education is possible in village, town or city because it transcends surroundings, be those rural or urban. Quality education is just as important for our neighbour's children as it is for our own. It makes no difference whether the parents are Catholic or Protestant, Muslim or Jew, Sikh or Hindu, Buddhist or Baha'i, atheist, agnostic or humanist. It is just as important for children of the rich and children of the poor; for the advantaged and the disadvantaged; for the able and the disabled; for boys and girls.

Every country needs a healthy society, a society that hums with activity and vitality. That in turn generates a vibrant economy where new ideas and practices result in increased circulation of goods, services, and monies. Change becomes the constant as the old is regenerated or replaced by the new. Expectancy, welcoming the new, is glad to leave the outworn and obsolete. This does not lessen an affection and attachment to fixed principles and does not weaken family and community ties. It strengthens them by looking for new ways to further their richness. An emphasis is placed not so much on the material aspect of change as on the more spiritual, the intangibles that create and stabilize change – intangibles such as honesty, openness, freshness. This renewal does not discard older people; it encourages regeneration throughout life and makes use of ageless talents and abilities, with individuals respected not for their age but for their on-going vitality and contributions.

Each nation prospers or declines depending upon the education of its children. Civil, religious, political, legislative, judicial, and economic reforms continue only through that education. The future of humanity lies, therefore, not with adults but with children. Children are always the hope of humanity; education is always the avenue through which that hope comes to fruition.

Education in its purest form is a gradual process of awakening individuals to their unlimited potential for good. It is unhurried, unpressured, unfettered. It resembles the unfolding of petals in a flower. It simply requires the right atmosphere and nutrients. Nature supplies those for the flower; parents and teachers supply those for the child.

The awakening occurs through growth in all facets of the individual – what has been termed the whole person. While many people have talked about educating the whole person, few have actually done so because the whole has never been clearly defined. Most thinkers have limited the whole to the physical, mental, and social dimensions. Others have included the emotional or creative or moral realms. A few have included the spiritual. And fewer still have included all these facets. As a result, the curriculum in almost all public schools has been designed to encourage growth in only a few of these dimensions, and often with exclusive focus on intellectual growth. Progress of children and predictions of their success have been based almost solely on intellectual performance. Generations of children have suffered from this narrow focus.

It is not intellectual development alone that governs progress but the development of all dimensions of an individual. *All* activities carried on in the school, from the purely academic through the artistic to the broadly practical, contribute to growth in these dimensions.

These dimensions are not discrete. They blend with each other within every individual – some facets more highly developed than others. Development here is always a life-time process. Development begins in the home, is reinforced in the school, and beyond that continues only through individual initiative.

Fulfilment of potential depends solely upon the individual's continuing growth in all facets. Growth is never-ending; fulfilment is never-ending. Both are always relative – relative to where one was, one is, and where one is pushing towards in expression of the moral, mental, emotional, physical, social, creative, and spiritual dimensions. In the school setting children are helped in that growth and fulfilment through example, encouragement, effort, and receptivity.

Every child is always at a different level of expression of these dimensions from every other child. It is the parent's responsibility and the teacher's job to discern as well as possible those levels and to encourage each child to build upon and enlarge that expression. That building or enlarging is the growth that forces the individual to use his or her potential.

Major responsibility for such growth rests with the individual student and home, but the school supports the growth by providing an atmosphere and activities which, when undertaken seriously and conscientiously by the student, contribute strongly to this growth, which is, in the final analysis, unfoldment of character.

The unfoldment is what enables students to become confident, considerate, and intelligent contributors to society. And that contribution will be in any walk of life students elect, one no less important than any other.

The educational philosophy or statement of fundamental belief (*see* Appendix A, p.101) should be the same for every school in the world. It becomes a permanent, solid foundation for the school and for every activity carried on by the school. Like a rock, it will withstand waves of change and time. Children, parents, teachers, administrators, support staff, buildings, grounds, facilities, technology, resources, and curriculum change, but the one all-encompassing philosophy remains fixed, permanent.

This philosophy can be effective only if all teachers, administrators, and support staff sustain it. Those who do not, undermine the effectiveness of those working to support it. Factions develop insidiously and students are torn between conflicting directions and practices.

Parents should also be supportive of the philosophy. Most will be. Experience has shown, however, that not all will be. Some will be supportive in word only. A few will openly work against it, either ignorantly or intentionally. Under the guise of volunteering or assisting, some parents sow seeds of criticism about the administration and teaching. Constructive criticism is healthy for the school and system; destructive criticism is unhealthy, and eventually poisons the atmosphere essential for the development of character. While major responsibility for the growth of the child rests with the home, especially in preparing the child to be receptive for learning, the home can seldom replace the comprehensive education essential for development of the educated citizen.

One of the most challenging tasks teachers and administrators face is maintaining an atmosphere which contributes to the total education of the children in their charge. It is a continuous challenge because there is always some individual, group, or agency that wants its own ideas spread within the system. Public schools do not exist for any special interest group or individual. They exist for the freeing of each student's potential. Teachers need to guard against the breaking down of their efforts and responsibilities to educate the whole child, and parents need to support the professionals trained specifically to educate their children.

CHAPTER 2

Standards for Teachers

Teachers teach what they are. Their mental states, like lifestyles, influence students more deeply than do intellect and ability. Behind the mask of many a pleasant guise lies mental, emotional, or moral weakness that manifests itself as deceit, dishonesty, domination, arrogance, sensualism, or an unhealthy ambition for recognition, position, and power. That is what influences students, not the pleasant manner.

The mask of pleasantness deludes the innocent and leads many an unsuspecting child into patterns of thought and activity which are harmful to growth. Many deluded young people never do gain release from those patterns. Some are mentally, emotionally, morally or socially crippled indefinitely. So it is not a pleasant personality that is needed for teaching; it is an individual of outstanding character, – thoughtful, respectful, cooperative, principled. This individual, like any educated citizen, must be a problem-solver, a producer, a doer, a thinker. Without exception, teachers have to cultivate those qualities that make for the truly educated citizen. Growth will continue while the teacher is on the job, but the qualities should be evident before entry into teaching.

It is the job of the Faculty of Education at every degree-granting college or university, in cooperation with sponsoring schools and teachers, to screen carefully every teacher applicant. This screening must be more comprehensive and rigorous than that conducted for entry into any other field. It must include interviews of candidates and interviews of those who are familiar with their work, activities, and background. Mental and emotional stability, along with high moral standards, must be clearly apparent, and are best determined by those familiar with each applicant's work and history. Qualities of the educated citizen should be clearly apparent during training and development for the applicant to be certified to teach. Those doing the screening must themselves be of outstanding character.

Except in emerging or developing countries, where advanced education has not yet progressed to a significantly high level, admission to a Faculty of Education should be confined to those who have a bachelor's degree. This ensures an adequate level of scholarship for entry into teaching. Developing countries will have to grow to that level of entry.

Scholarship is important in every teacher, as are accomplishment and staying power. The crucial element in the selection of a teacher, however, is the character of the applicant. Without teachers of outstanding qualities, character education of students in public schools is impossible. Every country can afford to have only the best in character educating – elevating – its children and young people.

CHAPTER 3

Standards for Students

Although I have had over twenty years of teaching experience, virtually all at the high school and university levels, and have seen many students go on to what appears to be productive lives, I was never satisfied with the focus of that teaching. Emphasis was always on student achievement and performance, largely academic, with little emphasis on thoughtfulness, cooperation, and integrity. Measurement of progress was based primarily on knowledge and skills, with some reference to work habits. These are important elements of education and have their rightful place, but that place should always be secondary to growth in character.

Character is the host of qualities that comprise each individual. There are as many combinations of those qualities or attributes as there are individuals – literally billions.

Every person individualizes the qualities in unique ways, out of which should arise progress and prosperity, peace and goodwill. In far too many cases, the results are the opposite – poverty and lack of progress, war and ill will. Why? Because too many individuals are motivated by lust for power, prestige, or position. Individuals who are consumed by this self-aggrandizement may have attended school, college or university, but they have not been educated. They are enslaved by their own self-centredness, and need to learn that the universal qualities essential for the unfoldment of character and accessible to all should always be used in the interests of humanity.

These qualities enable one to see things from another's position; to work alongside others in spite of differences; to compromise; to refuse to react to resentment, animosity or disdain; to be patient with one's own and others' shortcomings; to persevere to a successful conclusion. These qualities are the foundation of human activity and ultimately the prime determiners of success in human affairs.

Educational progress can be determined more readily by assessing individual conscientiousness, perseverance, and thoroughness rather than by measurement of intellectual abilities.

Teaching for high levels of intellectual achievement and performance does not need to be abandoned. Nor does the assessing of achievement and performance. Assessment should continue. But emphasis should shift from intellectual achievement and evaluation to cultivation of the *qualities* essential for success. Paradoxically, experience shows that one of the results of that shift is enhanced achievement in all activities, – academic, artistic, athletic, and practical. What happens is that the exercise of the qualities gradually becomes natural and paramount and a high level of achievement eventually follows. The focus slowly shifts from performance or achievement to *living* of the qualities.

All schools are nurseries of character, places where growth takes place over many years. Growth cannot be rushed. It is the work of moments put together, one after the other, carefully nurtured so that there is no disruption of the gradual growth taking place.

Where there are disruptive students, that disruption must be stopped. This can normally be handled by the individual teacher. Where that is not possible or is not being done, and I have witnessed such situations, the administration needs to remove the disrupting students and ensure that they do not return to school until there is assurance that no further disruption will occur.

Removal may be within the school or it may be without. If students have to be sent home, that must be done. If privileges need to be denied, that too must be done. Physical restraint may be necessary in cases of severe behaviour problems, but physical punishment in any form should never occur. Yelling, screaming, and shouting are inadmissible. No admonishing of students in front of others should ever take place. Discipline should be consistently firm, decisive, and swift, but never humiliating or abusive. The dignity of the child or young person being disciplined must always be upheld, even in the most difficult of cases. In all cases of discipline, teachers and administrators should be encouraged to act as they would if they were kind, firm, and judicious parents. Character cannot be elevated by brute force or intimidation.

In some rare severe cases, such as violent attacks, police officers may have to be called upon to ensure the safety of students and staff. Because they are not educational but criminal issues, they require legal and police support for their initial handling. Crime must be checked immediately. Once that has been accomplished, redirection of a student can begin. The latter cannot precede the former.

In all schools, procedures need to be established for the orderly discipline of students. These procedures should include deprivation of privileges, removal from activities on a temporary or long-term basis, class suspension, school suspension, transfer to another school if possible, or expulsion from school if all efforts to assist reformation of character have been exhausted. Age is not a factor. Disruption at any age, including the first years of school, is unacceptable. Academic and practical studies can still continue outside the school, but character development is impossible until there is receptivity to instruction and a willingness to abide by school requirements. The basic purpose of the school is always elevation of character. Conduct is a vital part of that elevation.

Leniency with disruptive students leads to poor learning situations and therefore little growth in character development. Society suffers from this leniency because students are ill-prepared to contribute to society, not through lack of knowledge, skills, or career preparation, but through lack of character development.

Where students fail to fit in with school rules, they should be directed to work with school and peer counsellors, social workers, psychologists, health officers, elders in some cultures, and others in the community to help them improve their behaviour. There should be cooperation among home, school, and community personnel.

While many people feel education is a continuous process throughout life, and different countries establish differing starting and leaving ages for formal education, my own view is that institutional education is not necessary before six years of age. There should be no hurry to start school. Education is going on before this, but it is more informal and incidental. While difficult in many situations, parents should provide the direction for the children almost entirely prior to this age.

Childhood is a time for freedom from formality and highly structured institutions, a time for play and enjoyment of nature and home. No instruction is needed in the basics of reading, writing, and mathematics except in naturally incidental ways. Parents the world over should resist the pressures that inevitably accompany evolving complex technological and service societies to speed up the formal schooling of their children. The most important thing for young children is to feel the love that only caring parents and family can provide.

No student should remain in public school beyond the age of nineteen because school cannot help shape the character of individuals beyond that age. Each individual has to assume that responsibility alone from then on. Academic or career development continues with further formal study, but character development continues only with individual initiative.

I have seen many students linger in senior high school for academic and social reasons, but that lingering has almost always delayed their development. Serving primarily to reinforce previous patterns of thinking and behaviour, such lingering is not progress.

The popular belief that students and society benefit from retaining in school those who do not want to be there, who refuse to learn, and who attend only because the law insists they attend, is a belief without substance. In reality few of these individuals do profit, and society seldom. In the meantime many other students have suffered from their presence and adverse influence, with teachers expending time and energy futilely encouraging them to fit into the standards set for all.

The root of the problem with recalcitrant students is refusal to accept well-intentioned instruction. This lack of receptivity is a blight, a barrier to self-development. It eventually has to be overcome. That is not easy to do, but must be done.

Only by identifying the problem, recognizing its obstructive nature, and working on its dissolution can such students progress. Self-will has dominated their

thoughts, feelings, and actions for so long that they have
not been able to adopt more selfless ways. As a result
they have had great difficulty accepting any guidance.
Cooperation with anyone has been almost impossible.
Only when individuals are ready to yield – to admit the
existence of a problem, – can others help them to
become more receptive to instruction. This is always an
individual yielding, awakening. Then progress can begin.

High standards for students are essential. These must
go far beyond outstanding performance in school
activities, important as this is, to include exemplary
behaviour, in order to bring out the qualities of the
educated citizen, which are the keys to ultimate success.

CHAPTER 4

Curriculum

Curriculum is content. It is what students study and take part in to guide their growth in all facets of character development. The public school curriculum should be basically the same everywhere in the world.

Coupled with the basic curriculum is the construction of school buildings to ensure that children of similar age groups study, play, and work together in an atmosphere which contributes to their wholesome growth. The best arrangement for character development is to group into one set of buildings children from five or six years of age to ten; group into another set of buildings those from eleven years of age to thirteen; and group into a third set those from fourteen years of age to eighteen. These schools can be termed the Primary School, Middle School, and High School respectively. Grade designations are Kindergarten or Grade 1 through Grade 5; Grade 6 through Grade 8; Grade 9 through Grade 12.

Although these distinct divisions result in higher capital, operating, and maintenance costs, they need to be made for the benefit of the children. The primary benefit is in ensuring an atmosphere which is appropriate for each distinct age group. In these divisions children are in constant contact with those of their own age group and interests. This encourages children to remain children as long as possible, an essential element in the development of character.

In some countries and in some isolated areas with small populations these divisions may not be practical or possible. All the children in such communities may have to be educated together in one set of buildings. That is a practical matter that has to be determined by state and local authorities. It needs to be kept in mind, however, that the divisions identified here provide the best physical arrangement for the different age groups. It also needs to be remembered that there is nothing going on in a community, isolated or non-isolated, small or large, more important than the education of its children, so provision for that education should be the first priority within every community. If school divisions as identified here are possible, strong efforts should be made to arrange for appropriate buildings.

Pressure from popular opinion will inevitably be brought to bear upon those responsible for the governance of public schools to admit children younger than five years of age. That pressure should be resisted. My experience shows that the later the entry into the formal curriculum, even up to seven or eight years of age, depending upon the child, the easier the transition from home to school. This is especially so for the child who has been immersed in love and affection and provided with a stimulating home atmosphere. Where these are lacking, school cannot completely overcome that lack. Good day care centres, fostering love and affection without a structured curriculum, can help overcome that lack to some degree.

Entry into school should take place at only one time of the school year for all students. Dual entry (at the beginning of a school term and halfway through a term) or continuous entry (monthly entry or birth date entry) are detrimental, as relationships are usually stabilized at an early stage of each school term. Even school transfers during the school year tend to upset those relationships, relationships so vital to children in their early and late childhood years.

It is also my view that the first year of school, whether at five years of age or six, should be a full day. The full day should be introduced gradually, from three hours a day to five over the first two months of school. Children readily adapt to routine and even at five years of age are capable of adjusting to the full day. For the few children who find the day too long, exceptions should be made to give them partial days.

Children do not necessarily need to enter Kindergarten. The majority of children can readily enter school directly into Grade 1 at six years of age. The more time children spend in a loving, enriching home with their parents prior to entering schools, the richer the school experience.

The Kindergarten curriculum should be centred on wholesome activity, including an abundance of music and dance and art; running, leaping, skipping, and climbing. It should also include listening to and telling stories, sharing experiences, and visiting relevant local areas. Use of radio, television, computers, and advanced technologies is important even at this early stage. The teacher's affection for every child should permeate the activities.

There is no need to force children to read. They grow into the ability to read at approximately seven or eight years of age. Some children will not be ready even then. Those who blossom later than others often attain highly developed skills and abilities in their own time. I met a thirteen-year-old, reading at the college level, who had not learned to read until she was ten years of age. An excellent teacher of English told me she herself did not learn to read until she was eight years of age. It cannot be emphasized enough that children should not be forced to read before they are ready to do so.

The Grade 1 to Grade 5 curriculum should focus on the children's national language and on mathematics. Language includes all facets of communication, such as listening, speaking, reading, and writing. Other areas of study and activity should include local history and geography, science, fine and performing arts, and physical activity. Local field trips enrich and broaden views even at this age if there is an educational focus. Work with computers and other technology is also beneficial as it builds familiarity and ease at an early age. Technological skill is not the aim, rather familiarity and comfort.

Twenty-five hours of instruction per week is adequate for children at this level. No home study is needed.

The curriculum for children in Grades 6, 7, and 8 (the Middle School years) should focus on the same subject areas as in the Primary School: first language, history, geography, mathematics, science, fine and performing arts, and physical activity. The only addition is a second language. The second language, introduced in the first year of the Middle School (Grade 6), and primarily conversational, should continue until Grade 11. In countries where English is not the first language, it should be the second language, as it will continue indefinitely to be the universal language in international commerce, diplomacy, law, politics, medicine, culture, communications, and education. Children without English will be at a disadvantage on the global scene. In countries where English is the first language, the second language of study will depend upon national and state preferences. Aboriginal languages may well meet the local need in this area.

At this level and even into High School the best approach for the furtherance of knowledge and skills is to concentrate on distinct subjects rather than to blend them. There is always some overlapping and intertwining of subjects. This blending is done through the study of topics, themes, or major ideas, looking at them from the perspective of the humanities, sciences, practical or fine and performing arts. This approach may meet the need of some students for a linkage of subjects, but as students develop analytical abilities, they naturally do their own interdisciplinary blending.

Organization for instruction in the Middle School should be subject-based, similar to High School with the exception that it should not be semestered. Year-long seven-or-eight-subject instruction is more beneficial for this age level than the more fragmented High School instruction. It provides for longer time with fewer teachers.

Again, twenty-five hours per week of instruction is adequate in a 195-instructional-day school year. If home study is needed, no more than sixty minutes per day should be assigned.

In Grades 9 through 12 (the High School years) all students, regardless of intellectual proficiency, need immersion in several areas. These include the national language (4 years); history and geography (3 years); mathematics (3 years); science (3 years); physical activity (3 years); and religious studies (3 years). Instruction in religious studies, which should begin in Grade 9, should be only for appreciation and understanding of the world's religions. There should be no indoctrination, proselytizing, or religious exercises. As well, elective or optional subjects should be offered in all four High School years in practical areas such as business, home economics, technical studies, computer studies, and the arts.

All students need academic subjects all their school

days. Exposure to ideas and views brought out in these disciplines, especially in the humanities, is essential for development of the whole person. Depth of examination varies widely from one student to the next, but examination and exposure are imperative for expansion of thought. Students with little interest in academics and more interest in the practical, artistic or vocational can study and acquire skills and knowledge in these latter areas, but need to accompany that with purely academic studies. Work experience, pre-employment, and career programs are not substitutes for academic studies.

Non-academically inclined students have important views and feelings on significant issues. They may well have advanced views on fairness, justice, mercy, and compassion. They need the opportunity and skills to bring these out for public benefit. The least articulate today may become the most advanced thinkers of tomorrow. These individuals often spend years struggling to articulate their innermost thoughts and feelings, so they need all the encouragement society can give them at each stage of their growth. Public schools should be the principal avenue for that encouragement in those early stages.

At this level instruction should be given for thirty hours per week – six hours per day for five days. All High Schools should operate on the semester system, enabling students to take twelve courses over a two-semester year. This will allow them to take forty-eight courses over the four years of high school.

Acceleration through the system should not be permitted. The basic purpose of education is not academic, artistic, athletic or practical acceleration and achievement; it is character development. And that is impossible to accelerate.

Home study should be no more than ninety minutes per day in the first two years of High School and no more than one hundred and twenty minutes per day in the final two years. A school year of 195 instructional school days is adequate.

Textbooks for the basic curriculum should be of the highest calibre possible at each level. Literature should be selected that elevates rather than entertains. Arguments that some students are incapable of dealing with ideas from outstanding literature and art are unfounded. They will take from those ideas whatever they consider important; those ideas will come back to them years later when needed. Shakespeare's observation that "a friendly eye could never see such faults" has just as much relevance in the market-place as it has on the floor of the United Nations, and is just as relevant to the common person today as it was when written centuries ago.

Textbooks, workbooks, manuals, curriculum guides, and other resource materials, especially in the sciences, need constant up-dating to keep abreast of the times. It should be the responsibility of state ministries of education to ensure such up-dating on at least a ten-year cycle, with at least one curriculum area up-graded each year. All technology must be kept abreast of contemporary practice. Students need the latest in ideas and practices so they remain on the cutting edge of world thought.

The curriculum may have to be modified for some students. These students are those who have major difficulty studying the prescribed content. Students with severe learning disabilities should never have limits placed upon their capabilities. No one knows when they will burst forth. The expectation and opportunity to do so must always be present, and wherever possible their education should take place with all other students. The curriculum modification, therefore, is not to replace the prescribed courses but to tailor their content to meet the current needs of the students. The regular courses can be undertaken when students are ready.

Curriculum for the gifted, those who show peculiar gifts for learning either academically, artistically, athletically or technologically, should be similar to that for all students, with the added opportunity to explore ideas and practices that challenge their special abilities.

Of all the areas within education that have proved to be vexing, none has been more so than the schooling of intellectually gifted children and young people. Parents, teachers, and administrators have relentlessly insisted that these students should be accelerated through the curriculum. Test scores have shown that they are superior to others in mathematics, the sciences or language. The solution, it has been claimed, is therefore to advance these students to higher grades to keep them from boredom. This practice fails to encourage development of the total individual.

What actually happens when children and young people are pushed or pulled outside their age group is forced intellectual performance but with a lag in development in a host of areas usually defined as the emotional, social, moral, and spiritual. Those areas are neglected or ignored and suffer as a result. Pressure for more advanced performance quickly becomes self-imposed and subtle, seen by no one, but felt by the child or young person. In many cases the individual feels outstanding achievement is expected and silently struggles to satisfy the expectations, giving the appearance of performing naturally, but inwardly experiencing gnawing self-doubt with regard to the appropriateness of social interaction, emotional responses, and ethical decisions among more mature students.

With rare exceptions, the imbalance will eventually result in great harm to the individual. Every accelerated student I have been familiar with – over thirty – has failed to achieve anywhere near his or her potential as a result of an imbalance in development. The child or young person has not grown emotionally, socially, creatively, morally, spiritually, or even physically, at the same rate as forced intellectual growth has taken place. Some individuals are overcome by their inability to cope with emotional issues, personal relationships, moral dilemmas, spiritual ignorance, creative vacuums. Some of them, overwhelmed by self-doubt, discouragement, and depression, give up struggling to gain their dominion over these burdensome feelings, and fail to use their remarkable abilities. A number become satisfied by performing menial tasks simply for peace of mind. Others commit suicide because they have been unable to cope with the expectations placed upon them. Others simply cope intellectually but without emotional control.

Intellectual development does not guarantee the ability to deal with things other than on an intellectual level. Intellect is not the key in dealing with life's everyday affairs. The keys are spiritual – the love of the good; and moral – the awareness of what is right and wrong and a willingness to live in harmony with what is nearest right. The spiritual and moral show us the need for development of the intellect, but the intellect does not tell us of the need for development of the spiritual and moral. On the contrary, it argues solely for its own self-importance without any need for spiritual and moral considerations. This is a major reason why so many adults with a highly developed intellect do not bring solutions to the world's problems that demand moral courage, justice, bravery, mercy or compassion. They have looked at the problems only from an intellectual standpoint.

One of the truly damaging effects of accelerating the

gifted is leaving them with the delusion that they are superior, a horrible belief to inflict upon children and young people. The fact is *all* have unlimited abilities. That has to be proved in everyday life, but the lack of its manifestation does not lessen the fact.

Forced acceleration is similar to cutting open the cocoon surrounding the larva, removing the organism's opportunity to strengthen itself by winding its own way out of the cocoon. It eventually dies before reaching its ultimate state as a beautiful butterfly. Individuals need to wind their own way through daily challenges at their own rate. This strengthens them.

The gifted need more assistance in the curriculum than any other group, as they have more to contend with than others. Because they can solve problems readily, they are given greater responsibilities, thereby placing further demands on them. On the other hand, others frequently avoid them because they do not readily fit in with the often tedious mental wrestling that goes on with less perceptive individuals. These gifted individuals usually have therefore a lonely path to walk. They often seek out friends who are less than sterling because they are a relief from the demands placed upon them. This in itself leads to great danger as some are readily led into situations they would not normally choose had they developed in a more balanced manner. A highly developed moral sense, for example, would give them the strength to protect themselves from potentially dangerous situations.

It is, therefore, not more challenges in their own fields they need, but more consideration from others, more affection, more understanding, more acceptance of their uniqueness; they need more solitude, more time to reflect upon things of their own choice.

In terms of the school curriculum, then, these students do not need extra stimulation. It is actually the less than gifted who need that. The gifted stimulate themselves with their own thoughts. The best thing in the curriculum for them is time to explore, to reflect upon, and to examine in more depth, the things other students are studying. Knowledge and skills they quickly pick up with others. Exploration in the school library, study of another language, enrolment in correspondence courses or distance learning, immersion in computer applications, or any activity to further interests, cultivate reflective skills or broaden outlook is appropriate *if without pressure*. The challenge here is to withstand the pressure from parents and others to force them into these activities. The logic of events in the years ahead will place enough demands upon them where they will be able to make use of their talents – in their own time, in their own way.

I am convinced that what would be most beneficial for all students is the understanding that there is a divine source of all intelligence and capacity, commonly called God, and that they and all others have the ability to express that intelligence in whatever they are doing.

This spiritual discernment brings with it humility.

Children should learn from an early age not to set themselves above or below others for any reason. Neither should they overlook the fact that some individuals run faster than others, some read with more understanding than others, some solve problems with more precision than others, some make wiser judgments than others. They should also learn that those human facts do not prevent them and others from running faster later, reading more intelligently later, solving problems with precision later, making wise judgments later. Neither does this discernment interfere with a student's effort to excel. That effort should always be exerted, but without fear of failure or anxiety if excellence is not forthcoming.

Without an understanding of the divine, students are too easily caught up in the clamour for haste and achievement that characterizes so much of the world scene. It is not, however, the school's responsibility to provide instruction in that understanding. That belongs entirely to the home and church, mosque, synagogue or temple. In this area, the only responsibility of the school is to maintain an atmosphere which supports the efforts of the home and religious bodies of all denominations to encourage their children to apply that understanding throughout the curriculum and in all school activities.

For character development, the only other area of the curriculum that needs to be addressed is values, the ideals cherished by society that need to be furthered by each generation for stability and progress. I believe everyone in a democratic society would agree on the necessity for such values as honesty, integrity, openness, dignity, self-worth, respect, care, peace, goodwill, freedom, and love. These values need to be clearly identified and consistently promoted and upheld. Then when the students go out into the world, they will take those values to better the world. The key here, of course, is to ensure that teachers, administrators, and support staff live the values – throughout the school and their own lives.

Acceptance of these universal values precludes retaliation – including withdrawal of services or work stoppage, revenge or recourse to violence to correct wrongs and injustices. Right adjustments should be made through due process of laws, rules, and regulations, all disputes settled by appropriate grievance procedures, labour courts, negotiation, conciliation, mediation, and arbitration.

Neither business nor labour interests should dominate the public school curriculum. Courses on business, labour, management, government, and other aspects of the economy may be offered, but they are peripheral to the academics, the arts, and athletics. Public schools do not exist to prepare young people for specific jobs. They prepare them for all markets, trades, and professions by encouraging development of the educated citizen.

It is the responsibility of business and labour to train young people *on the job*. In some of these jobs, government assistance may have to be provided. Partnerships among business, labour, and government are appropriate in the business world, but inappropriate in the schools. Public schools exist for the development of character, not for the development of careers.

Curriculum related to racial and ethnic groups can also be readily introduced. Courses and activities in these areas can be offered in addition to regular requirements.

Countless racial, ethnic, language, and religious groups demand that governments establish separate schools solely for their own group, with their own curriculum. I believe it is far better for their children and for society that they educate their children in the world's public schools. Parents and others can still preserve their own traditions, customs, religious views, and practices by providing for them in the home, community, church, mosque, synagogue or temple. If parents' beliefs are strong enough and their children are taught to love and live them, even in the face of strong pressure to abandon or compromise them, children should become strong enough to preserve them. If they fail to do so, it illustrates either a weakness of teaching, a weakness of learning, or a weakness of character. All public schools can establish an atmosphere which enables children and young people to test the efficacy of their cultural, personal, and religious beliefs and practices through the school's curriculum and focus on character development.

The beauty of the public school is that it brings together as no other system does children from diverse walks of life, religion, philosophy, and belief. Children learn at home and elsewhere that they are special, but learn in school through daily study, play, and work with others of differing views and social standing that *all* are special, and learn of the need to live cooperatively, respectfully, thoughtfully with others.

This schooling, rightly practised, protects against racial, ethnic, religious, and social prejudice, discrimination, and hatred. The beauty and power of public schooling, experienced over many years, produces love and respect of one another.

Should the curriculum include sex education, drug and alcohol education, tobacco education, gang education, health education, career education, life-styles education? It is impossible in public schools not to deal with society's preoccupation with these areas. The questions arise then as to *how, when,* and *where* these areas can be addressed reasonably to meet the needs of children and young people, families and society, and at the same time accommodate wide diversity in family moral, spiritual, philosophical, and personal beliefs and practices. This is best accomplished by having knowledgeable school counsellors present factual information in each area, encourage students to examine the facts through the prism of the standards expected of the educated citizen, and then leave students and parents to deal with the ways in which they wrestle with sex, drugs and alcohol, tobacco, gang involvement, and dangerous life-styles. Matters of health, hygiene, and personal problems are best left to counsellors and school health authorities to deal with on an individual basis. Information supplied here needs to be in keeping with family wishes. Sex education should be confined to its physical aspects, and birth control information provided without advice on its use. The moral, spiritual, emotional, and social dimensions of sex should be left to the home and church, mosque, synagogue, and temple, or any other community organization that families refer to for direction.

The school can begin with this part of the curriculum in Grade 6 and continue it until Grade 11. Provision must always be made for those parents who do not want to have their children taught by the school in any of these areas. The best way is for the school to provide parents with relevant information and encourage them to give direction to their children at home, screened through their own beliefs and practices. Under all circumstances the school must respect the right of parents and their children to work out their own approach in these areas. The effort of teachers, administrators, and support staff to uphold high moral standards in their own lives will do more to promote healthy practices in children and young people than all their counsel and advice, however well meant.

Instruction in these areas should not take away from the basic curriculum. One block of time in one semester in each of Grades 9, 10, and 11 is adequate in High School; one block of time for half of the school year in each of Grades 6, 7, and 8 is adequate in Middle School. As students readily dismiss repetitious content, there should be little overlap of content from one grade to the next. As well, there should be a specific sequence in each of the areas examined, a sequence appropriate to the age level of the students being taught. While a state Ministry of Education should provide the basic content for all schools in its jurisdiction, schools should be free to make adjustments with regard to the content and sequence to meet local needs.

There is one final related program that needs careful monitoring to ensure it is furthering the unfoldment of character. This is the extra- or co-curricular program, so-called as it supplements or complements the basic curriculum. An extremely important program, it has as much or more influence in shaping the individuality of children and young people as does the basic curriculum. It is imperative therefore that all activities within that program – the arts, athletics, theatre, student government, clubs – be conducted with the fashioning of character in mind.

Several things must be in place here for appropriate development to occur. First, there must be emphasis on excellence. The activities are not for frivolity or for leisurely pursuit. Strong demands are needed for growth in staying power, singleness of purpose, obedience to rules and regulations, unselfishness, peak performance.

Peak performance helps individuals overcome beliefs of limitation, and provides an example to others to do the same. Limitations of all kinds need to be transcended. Extra-curricular activities are an outstanding avenue for doing this.

The second essential is to avoid self-aggrandizement. Singling out children and young people for outstanding performance can be damaging. The recognition often leads to self-centredness, which in turn inhibits overall development. Media publicity is particularly damaging in this regard. Many children and young people spend years, some a lifetime, working out of that self-absorption, a vexing constriction to growth.

Third, children and young people should remain within their chronological age group for almost all these activities, and in particular athletics, to help guard against individuals being forced into situations they are not ready to handle. So many children and young people, seemingly more mature than others of their own age and possessing talents and abilities far beyond others of their age, give the appearance that they are ready to deal with others of similar ability. The fact is they are not. Children should take part in almost all activities only with those of their own chronological age – born within the same calendar year. Exceptions are inevitable, such as when various age groups must come together for an entire school production or in isolated communities where numbers in each age group are small, but these exceptions should be rare.

Fourth, only teachers, administrators, and some support staff, those thoroughly versed in character development, should conduct extra-curricular activities. Many well-meaning parents and community members who appear to be good models to emulate and who long to direct, coach or supervise should not do so. The reason is that the school has no control and no assurance that they are conducting the activities in keeping with the high standards established by the school. Short courses on character education are insufficient to guarantee that parents and others are of the character desired. All teachers and administrators must take part in these activities and be responsible for them, with the assistance, but not control, of the parents.

Under no circumstances should an extra-curricular program begin before the first year of Middle School (Grade 6). Middle School programs should not pattern those of the High School, especially those of a highly competitive nature, such as athletics. Emulation of older students and their activities militates against children remaining children as long as possible. This does not mean that there should be no inter-school competition in the Middle School. It means that emphasis on recognition, awards, and championships should be significantly less than in High School.

It is essential to remember throughout the curriculum – basic and extra-curricular – that the curriculum is simply the avenue for development of character. Serious losses occur in that development if focus on the primary purpose of education is shifted to performance and the acquisition of skills and knowledge. Abilities, skills, and knowledge are to be taken out into the world and made practical by thoughtful, respectful, cooperative, and principled young people. The school and society should never lose sight of that aim of the curriculum.

CHAPTER 5

Autonomy in Teaching

One basic curriculum is essential for every school throughout the world. How that curriculum is taught, however, is an individual matter. There are as many ways to teach as there are teachers. Every teacher needs to work out through years of experience comfortable and effective methods of instruction. This may take at least ten years. Teaching effectiveness is determined not solely by student achievement and performance, important as these are, but also by character development. It is character that determines the use of abilities, so abilities and character have to be connected. While the student is ultimately responsible for character, the teacher needs to concentrate on that development in everything taught.

Much has been said and written about the learning styles of students and how teachers must provide for the wide variation in ways in which children and young people learn. There is some truth to those observations, and teachers may need to experiment with various methods for different students. Those methods of instruction may include recitation, choral-work, drill, memory, question and answer, discussion, debate, explanation, demonstration, experiment, observation, analysis, lecturing, hands-on use of technology, listening, viewing, mentoring, tutoring, team teaching, student-partner teaching or whatever other method seems appropriate to the age and development of children and young people. The important point to remember is that each *teacher* must decide what is appropriate. That professional autonomy must always be protected by school governing bodies.

It is also important that children accept and adapt to different teaching methods. Children have many teachers over the years. And beyond that, throughout life, they will be working with countless individuals who have widely differing approaches to learning. Children need to learn early to glean from each teacher whatever they can. Great character growth occurs as children learn to do this, especially in terms of flexibility, openness, and originality. A complaining, petty attitude, found even among children, gives way to a freer, non-critical thought receptive to the new and fresh. This in no way lessens the analytical abilities of children. On the contrary, children learn to look for the good in each situation and become highly perceptive, increasingly able to discriminate between the desirable and the undesirable, in academics as in other areas.

Where teachers fail to be effective in instruction, there should be a serious effort over a full school year to help them be effective. Assistance should be provided by no fewer than two of the teacher's colleagues from the same level – Primary, Middle School or High School.

School and district administrators may be invited to provide assistance but should not be involved in the evaluation at the end of that year.

The evaluation should be done by at least two other teachers from the appropriate level, with school administration and the teacher's representatives agreeing on the selection of the evaluators. They should consider effectiveness from the perspective of the total development of children and include all school activities in which the teacher has been involved. The basic questions to be answered by the evaluators are these: Has the teacher had a significant impact upon the progress of students, including achievement, performance, thoughtfulness, respectfulness, cooperation, principled behaviour? Has he or she been a model of the educated citizen the school is striving to graduate? If so, the teacher should be recognized as a fully certified teacher. If there is reasonable doubt, the teacher should be dismissed, with removal of the teaching certificate.

The purpose of teaching is to awaken students to their potential for good. That potential can be realized only as students grow in knowledge, skills, and character. It is the job of the teacher to help students in that growth. There is a major difference between being a teacher and simply a guide. The teacher must explain concepts, must demonstrate and illustrate them, and make them as practical and relevant as possible. The teacher can never be therefore simply a facilitator or leader or motivator or guide, someone setting the stage for children to learn on their own. The teacher is always an awakener and must therefore *teach*. This is very hard work and never ends. For this reason teachers need ample time for rest and renewal.

In a never-ending effort to awaken students to their unlimited potential, the teacher must give the same affection and attention to both the receptive and the unreceptive, never knowing when thought and feeling will awaken. Children and young people awaken when least expected. The teacher must always be ready therefore to nourish them when they do awake, with more affection and encouragement.

Teaching, then, is the principal activity going on within every school. It is individualized by each teacher. No one should interfere with that individualization. It is a fact that where there is teaching, there is learning; where there is little or no teaching, simply facilitating or arranging for learning, there is little or no learning, and what little learning there is may well be incidental, lacking specific direction and purpose. Students cannot be expected to learn on their own without clear direction. So even if there are first-rate buildings, facilities, resources, technology, administrators, and support personnel, unless there is an emphasis on teaching, learning will be minimal and children and young people will benefit only slightly from school. Most noticeable will be lack of character development. That should never happen. But if it does, administrators and teachers need to focus once again on teaching, with emphasis on character development.

CHAPTER 6

Rotation in Administration

A major shift must be made in the current relationship between administration and teaching in order to maintain a focus on character education within the world's public schools. Administration has tended to dominate public education at both school and district levels by maintaining a self-perpetuating hierarchy of district administrators, school administrators, teachers, and support staff in a descending order of perceived importance, control, and influence over the education of children. Its misplaced importance has evolved over many years as a result of administrators' views of their importance and the subtle but growing acceptance of those views by teachers, parents, and public. Administrators have claimed that the key component of successful schools and school districts is the administrative team, – at the school level the principal, vice-principals, and administrative assistants; at the district level the superintendent of schools or director of education, the secretary-treasurer or comptroller, and the district's management team of supporting superintendents, directors of instruction and directors of various operations – depending upon the size of the district.

Administrators and researchers claim that successful schools and school districts have at their helms administrators who give visionary educational leadership. Research continues to support this view simply because if schools and districts are not accredited or recognized as being successful, administrators are replaced until they carry out what more senior administrators identify for school boards as being successful. Such replacement is not leadership; it is merely implementation – carrying out of what others dictate or determine. My experience is that administrators are neither visionary nor educational leaders. In the many years I served in education, I met only one administrator I could call an educational leader. He knew clearly what was needed for children in terms of character and values and carried out everything for his school board that enabled teachers to fashion that character. All organizational and administrative recommendations and decisions were made from that standpoint. He was basically a teacher who ensured that administration served the teacher.

Education administrators are actually organizers, coordinators, and delegators. They are teachers who are taking time out from teaching to serve other teachers. At both the school and district levels they should be officers who carry out the directives of school boards and ministries of education. They should advise and recommend to these bodies and then carry out whatever these bodies decide. They should work closely with other teachers, students, parents, and community groups. They should work with these groups with sensitivity and cooperation. If they do their job as it should be done, they serve in fact as servants – servants to students, to parents, to the public, to teachers. They must first and foremost serve teachers, who in turn fashion the character of their students.

Administrators have seen themselves, however, as leaders of teachers rather than servants. Administrators give recognition to the importance of teaching, claiming that they themselves love teaching, but will seldom if ever return to teach on a full-time basis. They have in effect placed themselves above teaching. That is where the hierarchy started – in the minds of administrators. And practices of self-promotion, self-selection, self-perpetuation have cemented the hierarchy so that a true educational leader within the teaching profession, someone doing the thinking for the ages in terms of freeing children and society, someone wishing to broaden experience in the field, would have great difficulty getting an opportunity to gain administrative experience.

The emphasis on administration and its mythical nature as a leadership position, the steady flow of teachers out of teaching into administration as a permanent career, the payment of exorbitant salaries for administrators, and the lack of recognition of the importance of teaching, needs to be halted. Then a reversal of importance between teaching and administration can be made.

The solution is rotation in administration and a change in salary scales. With rotation, all teachers who qualify – those who are principled, efficient, well-organized, cooperative, energetic, experienced, knowledgeable, and dedicated to the development of character – can serve as administrators for a few years and then return to teaching. These individuals can readily serve as assistant principals for four or five years, serve as principals for another four or five years, and then return to teaching. Under no condition should any individual serve more than ten years in administration without returning to a full-time teaching position.

Those wishing to serve as school district administrators should apply only after having served as a school administrator and only after returning to a teaching position. School district administrators should never be appointed from school administrative positions. Appointment of administrators solely from teaching will emphasize the importance of teaching.

All district administrative appointments should be for limited terms. There should be no more than two three-year appointments for any position except that of superintendent of schools or chief executive officer. In that position a maximum of nine years should be established. In all cases individuals in these positions should return to a teaching position.

To ensure administrators and teachers do not confine appointments to their favorites, selection and

appointment of all administrators should be done by
school board members themselves. Board members
should conduct the short-listing and interviews, with
the advisory assistance *only* of the superintendent or
designate, a teacher representative, and a parent
representative. It is essential that there be no control of
appointments by the superintendent, any other
administrator, or any teacher. All qualified teachers
demonstrating administrative proclivities and a desire to
serve as an administrator must be given the opportunity
to serve. No personal, political, gender, ethnic, racial or
religious differences should interfere with this
opportunity. The willingness and ability to work for
character development in all children must be the chief
determinant in appointments.

The result of this rotation in administration is a
steady flow of teachers in and out of administration and
back into teaching. It is a healthy flow, bringing
freshness, newness, and regeneration to both
administration and teaching, with emphasis on the
teaching. All too often permanent administrative
appointments become a dam, an obstruction to progress.
Rotation in office removes the dam.

Whenever possible, school administrative selections
should be decided at least eight months in advance of a
new school year. This allows for appropriate transfer and
placement of teachers and support staff in an orderly way.

Salaries for all administrators, including district
administrators, should not be higher than for the highest

paid teacher. The teaching of children and young people is of far greater importance and value to the world than school and district administration, however complex they are claimed to be.

Rotation in administration will be strongly resisted because it will destroy the administrative hierarchy. Many in these positions will lose their control over the education of children and over others. As well, those aspiring for power, position, and prestige will not be able to look forward to them on a permanent basis.

A bold move needs to be made in this area. This one single revolutionary move will bring great freedom to the world's public education system and place accountability and importance in education where they rightfully belong – on the teacher, who in turn is freed to free his or her students. Freedom from oppression and suppression, freedom of expression and opportunity, freedom to satisfy aspirations, are inherent here for all teachers. The world's children will be the real beneficiaries as they become the focus of the increased freedom of their teachers. Then character development will truly flourish.

CHAPTER 7

$\mathcal{P}$arent $\mathcal{I}$nvolvement

To advance character education throughout the world parent involvement in schools needs to be clearly defined. Parents should concentrate primarily on preparing their children to be receptive to learning. This involves encouraging children to go to school every day ready to learn; sending them to school well fed, fully rested, cleanly dressed, studies completed; encouraged to look for the good in every teacher and activity; encouraged to take part willingly in school activities; encouraged to value the school and its role in helping the home to educate them. It also includes refraining from criticism of teachers and the school. This does not ignore real problems of the school. Those should be met openly and directly by parents and the school, but without embroiling children. Where these few obligations are met by parents, their children will benefit immeasurably. They will attend school daily, prepared to be receptive – ripe for growth in character.

Over the years some parents have tried to dictate what public schools should be doing. This has been particularly pervasive in the more advanced technological countries where virtually all parents have received relatively high levels of education and thereby consider themselves authorities on education.

The fact is, however, that mere attendance at school does not make an individual an authority on education. And it does not qualify anyone to have insight on how best to educate children. That insight comes only from hard-earned experience in teaching. And even with that experience, unless there has been a focus on the essentials of education – elevation of the mind and heart of every student – one may not become an authority. I recall teaching and coaching a number of students whom I later gave the opportunity to teach and coach others. They were able to teach the required knowledge and skills, but failed to awaken the students to their potential simply because they had not grasped the fundamental purpose of teaching. They were far from authorities on education. The same applies to parents educated in the public schools. They have been through the system, but may well have failed to grasp the spirit, the real purpose of the system – to awaken children to their potential.

It is therefore primarily the teachers and administrators working daily within the system who know what children need from an educational standpoint. Parents should do their utmost to support teachers in their challenging task of character development. They can do this best by supporting the school's efforts to educate the whole child; serve in a consultative capacity; freely and openly offer opinions on school issues; respect the professional judgment of teachers and administrators; supervise and chaperone on field trips and excursions; fund-raise when needed; assist in the organization and running of events such as book days, sports days, graduation ceremonies. Ideas from parents should be sought and implemented by the school where practical, but parental interference in the school's operation must be avoided.

The potential for parent interference in the school's character development of children is large. Many parents would like to become involved in helping children develop skills in academic and practical areas of the curriculum, in selecting personnel, in determining curriculum and school practices, in evaluating individual teaching methods, in controlling school meetings, in coaching athletes, debating teams or drama students. These are professional areas best left to the total direction of teachers. Parents should discipline themselves to take or send their children to school and leave them there alone with their teachers, unless experiences show parents that they must intervene for the protection and development of their children.

Where children do not have the benefit of conscientious parents to prepare them properly for school, social agencies, where they exist, in cooperation with the school, may well have to step in and provide the food, clothing, shelter, and encouragement that all children must have. The school must not have that responsibility placed upon it. The school has the major task that no other agency can successfully undertake –

the development of character – and must confine itself to that task. Social agencies such as health and welfare must assume the responsibility of sending neglected children to school ready to learn.

The public needs reminding periodically that teachers teach, children learn, and parents prepare their children to learn. And where parents fail to fulfil their obligations, someone else has to assume those obligations. The main reason for lack of growth on the part of children is parental neglect, which has nothing to do with the economic or social standing of parents but everything to do with insufficient love of the children. One of the most important things parents can do for the world is properly prepare their children for school. Parents do not have to teach, do not have to learn; they simply have to prepare their children for that learning.

Lack of food, clothing, safety, and shelter by parents who cannot possibly provide them for their children is not parental neglect. Where these conditions exist, state governments need to provide these basic essentials so parents can supply the love needed and help prepare their children for the learning that is as essential as the basic human needs of safety, shelter, and nourishment.

CHAPTER 8

Funding

In order to bring about the character development essential for individual, community, and world progress, adequate funds must be provided for public education. These funds should be funnelled through one major channel within every state, province or jurisdictional region – the state government governing each defined area within a country. While the federal or national government within a country should provide education funds for special circumstances, those funds should be given only to state governments so they in turn can allocate those funds as the state determines. States should guarantee full use and appropriate allocation of those federal funds.

Federal governments should not be involved in the governance of education under any circumstances. They can and should be involved in collecting funds, but should not determine or influence how those funds should be spent. Their primary purpose in supplying funds is to help ensure equity in education throughout a country. Some regions of a country, for example, may not have the economic or personal income base to support public education as well as other regions. It should be the job of the federal government in those cases to supply the funds comparable to those of the more financially well-off states. This practice is not a competition for federal funds; it is a practice to bring relative equity in public education to a country.

Specific areas for which federal funding may be required are directly related to federal initiatives such as immigration, language training, job training, skills up-grading, cultural and heritage preservation, protection of minorities, national assessment, equality of opportunity, gender equality, religious equality, political equality, racial equality, judicial equality. The addressing of these federal issues through public education must be left to local or state governments.

While federal governments may raise funds for public education through income tax, sales tax, value-added tax, or any other system which the people deem appropriate, the main system of funding for public education should be conducted by state governments. They should gather the needed funds through personal income tax, commercial property tax, residential property tax, sales tax, and an education tax.

Every citizen within a state should contribute financially to the public education of its children. This can best be done by state governments collecting through income tax returns 1% of net income from every citizen within the state. That tax, an education tax, must be used only for public education. All must pay this tax, including those who have no children and those who choose to send their children to private, parochial, denominational, dissentient, independent or separate schools. Public schools can readily accommodate all children, with complete funding supplied by the public. If some parents do not wish to have their children attend, and instead have them enrolled in non-public schools that is their right. But not at public expense.

Neither state nor federal funds should be provided to any private, parochial, denominational, dissentient, independent or separate school. The public has no jurisdiction, control or influence over those schools and therefore no funds should be provided for them. Every one of these schools exists to further its own religion, philosophy or way of life, and so it should, but financed only by those who wish to further those ideas and practices.

If any non-public school receives public funds, the state government should appoint members of the public to sit on its board of governors to direct the public interest in the use of those funds. The number of government-appointed members should coincide with the percentage of its operating funds coming from the public purse.

For those parents and others who have intense desires to send their children to non-public schools for a variety of reasons, deductions on personal income tax can be arranged for funds expended by parents for their children attending non-public schools. The same privilege should be extended to parents donating funds for public education for their children. This brings a measure of financial fairness to those intent on supporting non-public schools and at the same time ensure that public funds are not used to finance such schools, which should remain totally self-supporting.

Supporters of non-public schools argue that such schools save taxpayers money because taxpayers do not have to pay for children attending these schools. This is true. If these schools do not receive any public funds, the saving is the total amount it would cost to send these children to public school. If they do receive some public funds, the saving is the difference between the cost of a public education and the amount funded out of public funds for non-public schools. While economy of resources is important, it is secondary to the education of children and young people. And there is no system comparable in terms of character development to that provided by the world's public schools, however costly. So it is not a matter of saving money; it is a matter of using it wisely.

State legislation should be in place to ensure that local boards of public education cannot do their own taxing or fund-raising for capital and operating costs. State and federal governments alone must be the fund-raisers. And the state government should ensure an equality of financing and educational quality throughout the state. Local taxation and fund-raising through referendum or petition or direct taxation only works to produce an inequality in funds, services, and programs.

And if private businesses, large or small, wish to provide funds for schools, that should be done by giving those funds either to the local school board or to the state. The local board or the state will then allocate those on an equitable basis where the need is greatest. Otherwise schools with business bases and those with aggressive fundraisers bring an imbalance to regions, districts, and schools. All schools, even those in poorer areas, must have the best in terms of buildings, facilities, and equipment. Isolated areas of a state have children who need the same opportunity for character development as do urban and suburban children.

How much money is to be collected from the people and how much is to be spent on public education is a matter to be worked out according to regional conditions. This will vary widely depending upon the availability of monies, which depends greatly upon global, national, and state economies. A reasonable guide is to set aside 25% of state revenue for public school education. This would include capital, operating, and debt reduction expenditures. This would also be apart from monies set aside for post-secondary education.

The percentage of federal revenue for public education to be channelled to states would depend greatly upon the policies in effect at the federal level. Wide ranges in percentage could be expected here, depending also upon the stage of development of each country. Those still in the developing stages may well

have to allow for greater percentages for public
education than more highly developed countries.

While the tendency will be to compare one country
with another in terms of revenues, expenditures, and
salaries, this should be avoided. It is never a question of
monies with regard to quality of character development.
It is always a question of quality of teachers dedicated to
the task of character education regardless of funds or
lack thereof. The onus on state governments and local
school boards therefore is always to ensure outstanding
character in a nation's teaching force. First rate salaries
for teachers and first rate working conditions according
to state and national standards are imperative. Buildings,
facilities, equipment, and resources can be financed in
due course.

Provision must also be made for continual renewal
and replacement of all buildings, facilities, and
equipment, a never-ending task. Modernization and up-
dating are important for all schools and districts. This
encourages children themselves to keep abreast of the
times and keep thought focused on the new and
contemporary, which brings expanded horizons and new
possibilities. This is a vital part of character
development.

CHAPTER 9

Politics and Religion

Two of the greatest dangers to public education and its role in the development of the educated citizen are politics and religion. It is essential to understand the dangers and protect education from these influences. Both politics and religion can infiltrate public education and adversely influence the education of children. Because they both produce subtle hierarchical and oppressive practices, children become submissive to the system, and, except for those who do their own thinking, unknowingly perpetuate the hierarchical system. The result is stifled thought: an inability to openly question, to openly discuss, to openly debate; an inability to challenge authority or established practice; in sum, an inability to play an effective role in a truly democratic society – a society characterized by government at all levels which furthers rule of the majority with respect and protection of the rights of the minority, government that fosters widely diverse views and practices, government, in the words of Abraham Lincoln, "of the people, by the people, for the people."

Of the two dangers to public education the greater danger is religion. The religion referred to here is monolithic religions dominated by clergy who insist, openly or subtly, that their beliefs permeate and their followers occupy virtually all positions of influence and power within a nation. These religions, if not checked by the people, result in church states and state churches, suppressing any institution or practice that lessens their dominance.

The major problem with monolithic religion is that only those who subscribe to its beliefs are given freedom. Supposedly only they are the chosen of God. Those who do not subscribe to these beliefs are deprived of their freedom by being excluded from opportunities for advancement, and become lesser citizens, victims of the dominant thought. They have a place within the hierarchy of the education system, but it is always under the control of those in positions of power and influence. They are quite unknowingly oppressed, suppressed, and repressed. The system perpetuates itself and the ultimate sufferers of this domination are the children. Few children can come out of such a restrictive education as free, creative or imaginative thinkers.

To ensure freedom for a nation's people and the sound education of children, church and state should remain forever separate, and religious liberty for all guaranteed in constitutions, courts, and human affairs. All religions, from the bizarre to the common, from the smallest to the largest, must be allowed, within the bounds of law and reasonableness, to rise or fall on their own merits. Time and education will determine the longevity and effectiveness of each religion.

Ironically, religion should offer the world, and education in particular, its greatest promise. It should allow all children, regardless of religious or lack of religious background, to develop their potential. Religion is an explanation of the divine, showing what God is, how God governs, and how man relates to God. As people come to understand and appreciate this spiritual sense of things, the human begins to pattern the divine and there appears in human affairs greater peace, law, order, and goodwill. Oppression, suppression, and repression gradually dissolve and individuals are left to work out their own destiny and place in the human scene – alone with God and conscience.

This type of religious thought is the basis for all human progress. It results in true democracy. So where theocracy now exists, it will ultimately have to be replaced with democracy. Where neither theocracy nor democracy exists, people in those regions should grow gradually directly into democracy and avoid the suffering of passing through a theocracy and generations later into a democracy. All their institutions need to be run on a democratic basis, which should include provision for universal public education – essentially universal character education.

The watching that needs to take place in public education with regard to religion, then, is to ensure no domination of the public system by any religion. Unless guarded against, religious domination can occur rapidly through the appointment of teachers, administrators, and support staff with overwhelming numbers from a particular religion. Particularly true in positions of authority and influence, infiltration can occur where governments, school boards, and management consultants recommend or appoint likeminded staff. Governments and school boards need to encourage diversity of religion in appointments. Personnel or human resource departments need to strive to maintain this diversity.

Public schools must never be used to further denominational teachings. No religious literature of a denominational nature should be distributed by the schools and no denominational or devotional exercises should be offered by the schools. Courses on religion, however, should be an essential part of the High School elective program, as they foster understanding and appreciation of the thinking and practices of others.

Growth in character for all children occurs best in a secular public school setting, where children learn that, regardless of religious background or lack of it, all are the same – offspring of the same divine Parent. All are equal, all working for the common good of one another where there should be no thought of who is the greatest, whose religion is right or the nearest right.

The truly secular public school system actually has more spirituality permeating its system than any religious school because it allows for the development of every child, free from indoctrination from any specific denominational belief, free from the belief that some

children are better than others, and free to practise
within the school the beliefs taught by the child's home
and church, mosque, temple or synagogue. The public
school becomes the testing ground for those religious
beliefs. It is imperative for the preservation of that
spirituality, therefore, that no religion dominate in any
public education system, a system dedicated to the
development of every child.

Politics is also a serious threat to public universal
character education. It is not quite the danger that
religion is because its presence is more readily detected
and more easily checked. Nevertheless it is a danger.
The politics referred to here is that carried on by bona
fide political bodies with specific platforms on
educational reforms. Some political bodies may set out
to change public education to fit in with their social,
economic, and military beliefs. In their view schools
should become the agents for change in these areas. This
may include involving children in peace marches,
banning of arms, raising money for the poor and
homeless, furthering family planning, birth control or
abortion, or saving the planet from pollution. It may also
include efforts to further privatization, entrepreneurism,
capitalism, communism, socialism or totalitarianism.
While all political views can be examined objectively in
the classroom, public schools are not avenues for the
furtherance of any particular political view.

Public schools must always remain politically
neutral. They exist to elevate character. That is above

and beyond politics. Political parties of any type – communist, socialist, capitalist – should be excluded by law from taking over the public education system.

The best way to keep public education free from both politics and religion is to have school board members appointed by the state government. The danger here, of course, is that the government in power will appoint only those who subscribe to its political views and that with every change of government there will be a corresponding change in political views on school boards. Also distasteful to many is that local citizens will not have the opportunity to elect those they wish to have represent them and thereby have a less democratic system of local government. These arguments are valid, but the need to eliminate politics and religion from public education and to ensure high standards in the appointment of all within the public education system outweighs these considerations. In some countries, the judiciary is so appointed, and for the most part remains impartial from the standpoint of politics and religion. I believe these appointments, if undertaken with great care, so that appointees are not government representatives but are representative of wide diversity in political and religious backgrounds, will ensure that impartiality and quality.

Election of school board members results in too wide a disparity in quality of members. Diversity among school board members enriches; disparity destroys. This disparity ranges from the sublime to the ludicrous in motives, morals, abilities, appreciation and understanding of public education. Public education has suffered seriously from this disparity. The result has been that many of the professionals within the system have been unable to focus on the essential purpose of education – the awakening of children to their potential. So a major change from elected to appointed should be made in the selection of those governing local school boards.

Well-educated board members who are successful in their own field of work should be selected carefully by each Ministry of Education. They must have high moral standards, independence of thought, freedom from influence of special interest groups, love of children, and love of public education as a fashioner of character.

Board members should serve for no more than nine years, reside in the jurisdiction served, and be parents of children attending public school in the same jurisdiction, at least when appointed. Every effort should be made to ensure there not be on any board of governors a majority of members from one political group or religion.

These appointed board members must then become responsible for the selection and appointment of all employees within their jurisdiction, encouraging the high standards needed to promote the development of character so necessary for the world's children.

CHAPTER 10

Ethics

Ethics in education is extremely important because it is here that children early learn what is right and what is wrong, reinforcing what is taught in the home and in the community. In school children learn this from their studies, their play, their student government, their contact with hundreds of others, but primarily from their teachers.

Ethics are standards of conduct, the moral principles by which individuals are guided. There is no human activity not touched by ethics. It is important therefore for children to learn what is right and what is wrong.

Teachers teach ethics by precept and their own example. They themselves must know what is right and what is wrong and must practise the right. Consistency in this practice is essential for their students. Teachers regularly meet countless situations calling for moral judgment, including plagiarism, cheating on assignments and examinations, stealing, lying, self-righteousness, condemnation, complaining about others and conditions, breaking of confidences and promises, violence, retaliation, revenge, hatred, jealousy, and personal conflicts. There is in fact little time in a day when teachers do not have significant moral decisions to make. So all teachers, whether or not they wish to be, are fashioners of morals in children and young people.

The teacher's example is a strong fashioner of children's morals but it must be accompanied with precept. Children, and even young people, need to be *told* what is right and what is wrong. Some, who may have been taught rules of moral conduct by their parents and their church, mosque, synagogue or temple, need little or no explanation. Others may have been taught virtually nothing and need considerable direction and explanation of why some things are appropriate and others inappropriate. Coupled with the discipline that the teacher must exercise where there is unethical student behaviour, such demands make a teacher's load heavy. It is not the number of children that creates the load; it is lack of receptivity to the moral direction.

High ethical standards are essential for character education. They determine in large measure the degree to which students become thoughtful, respectful, cooperative, principled; these standards determine their degree of flexibility, creativity, originality, inventiveness; they also determine the level to which children and young people develop their ability to think, to solve problems, to produce, to perform.

The relationship between morals and performance needs to be better understood. Ethics and morals are closely related to the development of individual potential. I discovered this relationship in my mid-teens when to my dismay I realized that my performance on the sports field varied in proportion to my moral level. If I lied to someone, cheated on a test, or was not completely honest, my performance on the basketball court, baseball diamond or track was poor and unpredictable, whereas if I lived in harmony with what I had been taught at home, church, and school, the performance was predictably good. Inconsistency in applying what I had discovered prevented me from using the insight effectively. Many years later, when coaching high school and college teams, I observed the same phenomenon with many of the players. I tried to explain it to some of them, but they had difficulty grasping the relationship between morals and performance. I did not pursue the explanation as I felt there was not enough receptivity to make the knowledge practical. There is, however, a definite cause and effect relationship here that relates to character development and the development of individual potential. It needs to be examined more deeply.

Ethical standards cannot be ignored or treated lightly and have to be addressed by every individual involved in public education. It follows that everyone in the public school system must possess high moral standards, including school board members, district administrators, school administrators, support staff, volunteers, and teachers.

Standards such as those identified here have been furthered by many societies over the generations. They need to have even wider acceptance by the generations of today and tomorrow. The following statement makes clear the standards expected of all within the system.

This school system encourages its employees and appointed officials to uphold high standards in all dealings with each other and in carrying out tasks. These standards include adherence to honesty, openness, forthrightness, friendliness, fairness, equality, sensitivity to feelings, freedom of expression, allowance for differences in points of view, and respect for all.

These standards exclude vengeance. Where injustices need to be corrected, this correction should always be carried out in peaceful, thoughtful, and merciful ways. Restraint of wrongs is necessary, but without harm to anyone.

This public education system exists to elevate students, to encourage all students to work towards fulfilment of their potential, and thereby make a contribution to the world. All within the system need to support that purpose consciously by maintaining high standards in dealings with everyone.

CHAPTER 11

Summary and Legislative Guide

It should be clearly apparent that there are specific elements that must be in place to establish and maintain a public education system that fosters character education. These elements include one definitive philosophy, one standard for teachers and students, one basic curriculum, autonomy in teaching, absence of political and religious interference, specific parent support, rotation in administration, adequate funding, an appointed board of governors, and high ethical or moral standards. Once these are in place they need to be maintained.

To incorporate these elements in law, state legislatures need to pass appropriate laws and regulations governing public education. In developed countries these may well have to replace current provisions. In less developed countries they may need to be the initial legislation. The laws and regulations need to cover only the areas identified here and a few others. These few other areas, which are important but have not been addressed here because they are not essential elements of character development, deal with services such as transportation, accommodation, buildings and grounds. Set forth in the following pages are guides to establishment of these laws and regulations.

Article 1 – Foundation

SECTION 1: *PHILOSOPHY.* A philosophy or statement of fundamental belief does not vary with local conditions or the idiosyncrasies of diverse populations. It should be the same for every public school: a clear statement that *all* education is the elevation of character. This elevation should involve every facet of the individual including the moral, mental, emotional, social, physical, creative, and spiritual. This philosophy should also indicate that major responsibility for the individual's education rests with the home and that the state and school support that responsibility by providing a curriculum and activities that allow for that growth in all these dimensions. Everything carried out within the state, district, and school related to education should be based upon that philosophy.

Every public school should prominently display that statement of philosophy for all to read. The importance of the philosophy can never be over-emphasized. Thorough examination of it will lead to resolution of the many difficulties that inevitably arise periodically in public schools.

Article 2 – Governance

SECTION 1: *MINISTER OF EDUCATION.* Every state, province, or county should appoint one individual to oversee the education of all children and young people within its jurisdiction. This individual should be known as the Minister of Education. He or she shall be college educated, have been successful in his or her field of work, have an appreciation of education, and have high moral standards. The individual appointed shall not remain in office longer than five years.

The Minister of Education should appoint separate directors to coordinate and supervise work in the following divisions: administration; finance; selection, training, and certification of teachers; curriculum; student services and standards; buildings and sites; non-public education. These directors should meet together with the Minister of Education not less than once every three months to monitor progress in all areas. Directors should not remain in office longer than four years. If a Deputy Minister of Education and Assistant Deputies are appointed, they shall not remain in office for more than three years. Continual revitalization of the system is essential for its health. Rotation in office ensures that revitalization and forces individuals to keep abreast of the times. These individuals need to be selected carefully by the Minister of Education to ensure diversity in religion, philosophy, and personal beliefs. High standards in professional and personal affairs must be evident in all those selected.

SECTION 2: *BOARDS OF GOVERNORS.* The Minister of Education shall appoint a Board of Governors for every school district within his or her state. These

individuals will be the sole governing body for each
district and must ensure the district keeps abreast of the
times in all educational matters. These people should be
carefully selected from the main community or
communities within the governed district. They should
not be selected for political, religious or personal
reasons. Board members shall be college-educated, be
successful in their own fields, have high moral
standards, be independent thinkers, free from the
influence of special interest groups, have a love of
children, and have a love of public education as a
fashioner of character.

Board members must, when appointed, reside in and
be a parent of a child attending public school in the
same jurisdiction in which the Board member governs.

Members of the Board of Governors must confine
their work to policy-making and not interfere with the
daily operation of schools. Operation of the schools
must be left to the district Superintendent of Schools
and appropriate staff. The following list of duties may be
helpful as a guide to new members of each governing
body: ensure that the school system keeps abreast of the
times in important educational matters; share leadership
in improvements with parents, students, teachers, and
administrators; be available for consultation with the
public, teachers, students, parents, and administrators;
acquaint the public and all within the system with
Board policies and proceedings of a non-confidential
nature; exchange ideas with other Board members on

important decisions to be made by the Board; help teachers maintain a high professional standing; be alert to the fact that the Board member's primary allegiance is to the public as a whole and not to any political, religious or special interest group; ensure that the Board utilizes federal and state opportunities for financial support; retain control of final decision-making with regard to policy and management of the system, but refrain from involvement in administrative details; be supportive of personnel carrying out Board policies; maintain strict control over all administrative appointments and not delegate appointments to senior administrators; ensure that Board policies are implemented appropriately, and ensure that practices arising from policies are evaluated periodically.

Meetings of a Board of Governors shall not be held without all members being notified and invited. If a meeting is held either officially or unofficially without all members invited, the Minister of Education shall be so advised. If after investigation this proves to be the case, that Board shall be dissolved immediately and a new Board appointed.

A Board of Governors may comprise three, five, seven, nine or eleven members, with a balance if possible among ethnic, racial, religious, and political groups. A balance should be maintained between male and female members, if possible. Terms of office shall be either two or three years. If the two-year term is chosen by the Minister of Education, Board members shall serve no more than four terms, to a maximum of eight years. If the three-year term is chosen, Board members shall serve no more than three terms, to a maximum of nine years. No Board member may be re-appointed to any other School Board throughout the state until the member serving his or her terms has been out of office for at least ten years. An appointment after a ten-year absence shall be for no more than two two-year terms or one three-year term.

If any Board member fails to carry out his or her duties, the Minister of Education shall remind that person of his or her obligations. If these obligations still remain unmet, the Minister shall immediately replace that member.

Recall of a member of a Board of Governors can be made by the Minister of Education after receiving a petition from at least 10% of the registered voters for a particular school district and after investigating the alleged problems and finding them to be valid. Any member so recalled shall not be appointed again to any school Board of Governors in the state concerned.

Article 3 – District Administration

SECTION 1: *SUPERINTENDENT OF SCHOOLS.* Administration of each school district within a state shall rest with a chief executive officer to be termed Superintendent of Schools. He or she shall be appointed by the local Board of Governors, and shall report to and be responsible to the Board of Governors of the district concerned. This individual shall also carry out any work assigned by the Minister of Education. Term of office for the position shall be two years for the initial appointment; and if proven satisfactory to the Board of Governors within those two years, re-appointed for a second term of three years; and if proven satisfactory to the Board of Governors within those three years, re-appointed to a final term of four years, for a maximum of nine years. After completing a full term as Superintendent, that individual must return to a full-time teaching position if he or she wishes to remain within the public education system.

An individual appointed as Superintendent of Schools must be college educated, have an appreciation of education, have high moral standards, have been a successful public school teacher and administrator, serving at least ten years as a full-time school teacher and at least five years as a school administrator. Also, no one shall be appointed Superintendent of Schools who has not served at least three years as a public school principal.

SECTION 2: *SECRETARY-TREASURER.* One Secretary-Treasurer shall be appointed by the local Board of Governors for every school district within a state. He or she shall report to the Superintendent of Schools and advise both the Superintendent and the local Board of Governors on all matters related to the financial and business operations of the district. The Secretary-Treasurer may be party to discussions and debates on educational issues within the district if the Superintendent of Schools or Board of Governors so decides, but he or she has no voice or vote on decisions to be made on education issues.

Term of office for the Secretary-Treasurer shall be a renewable three-year term. As this office requires some continuity and as it is a minor office with regard to impact upon the education of the children and young people, it is exempt from the principles of rotation in office and limited terms of appointment. If there is any interference by the Secretary-Treasurer in the harmonious and orderly operation of the school district, he or she shall be reminded by the Board of Governors to remain separate from the educational aspects of the district. If there is no immediate improvement in this regard, the individual shall be dismissed by the Board and replaced immediately.

Every Secretary-Treasurer must be college educated, have training in appropriate business and financial practices, have been successful in his or her field of work, have kept abreast of the changes in contemporary technology and accounting practices, have an appreciation of public education, and have high moral standards.

SECTION 3: *ASSISTANT SUPERINTENDENTS.* If the Board of Governors of a school district so decides, it may appoint appropriate Assistant Superintendents for the proper administration of a district. Assistant Superintendents report directly to the district Superintendent of Schools.

Appointments should be for three years with a second three-year term permitted if performance is satisfactory. No individual may be re-appointed Assistant Superintendent upon completion of six years until he or she has once again taught full-time in a public school for at least five years.

An Assistant Superintendent must be college educated, have an appreciation of education, have been a successful public school teacher and school administrator with at least ten years as a full-time teacher and at least five years as a school administrator. No one shall be appointed Assistant Superintendent unless he or she has served at least three years as a public school principal.

SECTION 4: *OTHER ADMINISTRATIVE OFFICERS.* A Board of Governors may appoint other district administrative officers to ensure the proper servicing of the district education system. These may include Directors of Instruction, Directors of Administration, Directors of Curriculum, Directors of Student Services, Directors of Special Services, Directors of Technology, and others. All of these positions must be for limited terms of office of four to five years and non-renewable except after a return to full-time teaching for at least five years.

No one shall be appointed Director of Instruction, Director of Administration, Director of Curriculum, Director of Student Services, or Director of Special Services without at least ten years of full-time public school teaching experience. And no one shall be appointed Director of Instruction without at least three years in school administration, where at least two of those three years have been as a public school principal.

Every school district, regardless of enrolment, shall have at least one Director of Instruction. There should be one Director of Instruction for every 15,000 students or part thereof.

Re-assignment of all administrative officers at the close of their terms shall be to teaching positions.

Requirements for all educational administrative positions are the same. These include a college education, successful public school teaching and administrative experience, an appreciation of public education, and high moral standards. Graduate study in related fields is desirable but not essential. The essential qualities for all administrators are a desire and an ability to serve – to serve teachers, students, parents, and education itself. It is a desire also to uphold the integrity of public education, an education that must remain apart from political, religious, and personal ideologies.

SECTION 5: *SUPPORT STAFF.* Every Board of Governors must select with care all district and school support staff. The main purpose of all support staff is to provide services for the smooth and orderly operation of the schools. All employees must be familiar with and supportive of the district philosophy of character education. They must be models of good character themselves, be cooperative with all, and have high moral standards. They must be competent in their field of work, be well-spoken, and have an affection for children and young people.

Article 4 – School Administration

SECTION 1: *PRINCIPALS.* All teachers within a school district who are qualified, who demonstrate the ability to be an administrator, and who desire to be an administrator, shall have the opportunity somewhere in their career to become a school principal. School administration does not exist without teaching. Teaching, on the other hand, survives without administration. It thrives though when supported and served by an unselfish administration.

It is imperative that teachers do not slip out of teaching to be lost forever in school or district administration, so the practices of rotation in office, limited terms of office, equality of the sexes, and equality of opportunity should be fixed by law and regulation. This will help teaching to remain the focus of all school and district activity.

SECTION 2: *DUTIES.* A Principal is responsible for the orderly and harmonious operation of a school. Duties include teachers' timetabling, teaching assignments, placement and promotion of students, supervision of curriculum implementation, textbook use, public relations, extra-curricular government, and any other duty assigned by the Minister of Education and the local Board of Governors.

The Principal is responsible for ensuring that the school is run on a purely democratic basis. This means that administrators and teachers work cooperatively for the sound education of the students, an education based totally on elevation of character. The Principal must consult with teachers on all matters affecting their work, and shall not interfere with their right to decide on their teaching style, their selection of authorized textbooks and resources, and their communication with all involved in the education of their students. Because ultimate responsibility for administration of the school rests with the Principal, the final decision on conflicting matters within the school must rest with the Principal. For resolution of irreconcilable differences teachers and Principal should consult with the district Superintendent of Schools. The ultimate decision on school-based matters shall remain, however, with the school. The parties involved need to work out their own solutions.

SECTION 3: *ASSISTANT PRINCIPALS.* In every school enrolling at least 100 students, an Assistant Principal shall be appointed. The amount of time spent on administration and teaching shall be determined by the Superintendent of Schools in consultation with the Principal of the school concerned. Duties of the Assistant Principal shall be determined by the Principal and shall include assumption of all the Principal's duties in his or her absence.

SECTION 4: *APPOINTMENT.* Principals and Assistant Principals shall be appointed by the district Board of Governors. The Superintendent of Schools, while gathering information on applicants for these positions, may consult with other administrators and any one else he or she may wish in order to get a full picture of the capabilities and character of those applying for these positions. The Superintendent or designate, a teacher representative, a parent representative, and the Board itself shall be the only members of the short-listing and interviewing committee for all administrative positions. The Board alone shall decide all appointments.

Equal opportunity must prevail throughout all appointments to ensure that every eligible teacher who applies for these positions realizes fulfilment as an administrator.

Individuals applying for appointment as Assistant Principals and Principals must possess at least the following qualifications: a master's degree in any field of study, highly successful full-time teaching experiences over a period of at least ten years, outstanding organizational abilities, a history of being firm, fair, and friendly with students, a record of being cooperative and friendly with others, be an independent thinker, be a tireless worker, have a large capacity for work, have demonstrated a willingness to serve, and have high moral standards.

Terms of office for both Assistant Principal and Principal shall be four to five years each. At the end of a term as Principal individuals shall return to a teaching position within the district.

Article 5 – Teaching

SECTION 1: *SELECTION*. Only individuals of outstanding character with a bachelor's degree from a recognized college or university should be eligible for admission to the teaching profession. Individuals wishing to become teachers must apply to a Faculty of Education established within an accredited state public university. It is the responsibility of the applicant to supply evidence of service to others, a history of high moral standards, a serious commitment to intellectual pursuits, an appreciation of and involvement with the artistic and/or athletic, and a willingness to teach others skills and knowledge in these latter areas. The applicant must be thoughtful, respectful, cooperative, and principled – a model of the educated citizen. Those providing references must comment on the applicant's expression of all these attributes.

Every Faculty of Education should establish at least a three-member screening committee of ethical people to investigate the background and eligibility of every applicant. Each committee must be given access to the applicant's university, college, school, and work records to determine the suitability of the applicant. Interviews may have to be conducted with appropriate persons to get a full and accurate picture. Interviews must also be conducted with each applicant prior to admission to the Faculty. All accepted must show promising proclivities as teachers of children or young people. No reason need be given for not accepting a particular applicant, and all information supplied by references and those interviewed shall be checked and shall remain confidential.

Once admitted to a Faculty of Education the candidate is expected to maintain high levels of conduct and performance. These individuals become very quickly one of the prime fashioners of a nation, and as such need to be models of the best society has to offer the world.

SECTION 2: *FACULTIES OF EDUCATION.* Every state should establish and maintain within an accredited degree-granting public college or university a Faculty of Education. Each Faculty of Education shall be staffed at the undergraduate level with the most outstanding practising teachers and administrators. They must have at least ten years of successful teaching experience in public schools. They must also have a record of service to their students, be skilful teachers in their own subject areas, be ideal models for prospective teachers to emulate, and have high moral standards. Appointments shall be for no longer than three years, at the end of which individuals shall return to their own teaching positions in the schools.

Faculties of Education are not academic institutions; they are professional institutions. Each Faculty of Education shall offer a two-year program, at the end of which successful candidates are granted the degree of Bachelor of Education. Programs for the elementary school and secondary school should be the same length. At least three months in each of the two years should be spent in teaching within state schools. While the majority of instruction within each Faculty of Education should be on teaching styles, techniques, and approaches, time must be provided for a thorough examination of character education and how it is achieved in practical ways within the schools. Each Faculty of Education should be viewed as a professional institution designed to prepare the highly qualified candidate – not in an academic way, which has already been done through college or university training – but in practical day-to-day teaching duties and assignments.

Selection of staff at the graduate level in each Faculty of Education does not have to be done as rigorously as that at the undergraduate level. As advanced work here is more on a technical and theoretical level in specialized areas such as curriculum, counselling, administration, special education, technology, and so forth, instructors and professors seldom fashion the thinking and feeling of their students to the degree done at the undergraduate level. Individuals selected here should be chosen more for their technical expertise than for their character, although that too should be of a high standard.

SECTION 3: *COLLEGE OF TEACHERS.* Every state should establish and maintain its own professional body of teachers, termed a College of Teachers. Each College should admit to its ranks those individuals granted the Bachelor of Education by appropriate colleges and universities. Each College should be governed by its own members, with advisory roles given to representatives of the Ministry of Education and each Faculty of Education within a state. The College shall not establish any rules or procedures that contravene state legislation governing education.

The purposes of the College are to certify individuals to teach, to ensure high standards of professional conduct, and to discipline its own members when necessary. Members of the College and the Ministry of Education are responsible for the financing of its operation.

SECTION 4: *RESPONSIBILITY.* Every teacher is responsible for the total education of every pupil under his or her instruction. This must include provision for moral, mental, emotional, social, physical, creative, and spiritual development. While attention is normally not focused on any single area at one specific time, an awareness and provision for growth in all areas are essential.

In school the teacher is the primary authority for pupils under his or her instruction. The teacher may consult with the Principal, Assistant Principal or other colleagues, but they do not usurp the teacher's authority to decide on the learning activities and the control and discipline of those pupils. If there is reason to question the teacher's judgment in these matters, the Principal must report to the Superintendent of Schools on that judgment, and have at least two other teachers investigate the areas of concern.

The school should inform parents of the standard of conduct and performance expected at all school functions. Teachers must be consistently firm, fair, and friendly in their dealings with all students.

Article 6 – Curriculum

SECTION 1: *SCHOOL ORGANIZATION.* The ideal organization of schools to further character education should keep students together within a broad chronological age grouping. The ideal is to have

Kindergarten or Grade 1 through Grade 5 in one group of buildings (Primary School); the next group from Grade 6 through Grade 8 (Middle School) in another group of buildings; and the third group from Grade 9 through Grade 12 (High School) in a third group of buildings. This gives broad, relatively compatible, age groupings of 5-10, 11-13, 14-18 years of age. This arrangement helps to have children remain children as long as possible by constant contact with those of their own age and interests.

SECTION 2: *CURRICULUM*. It is important to remember when establishing the curriculum for all these age groups that it is simply the avenue for the development of character. The curriculum needs to be content-filled. The teacher explores the content in keeping with the abilities of the children taught. There is no need to rush into that content nor speed through it. For growth in skills, knowledge, and appreciation, movement through all content should be gradual, unhurried.

Emphasis on gradual movement does not rule out the use of examinations and assignments to determine levels of skill, knowledge, and appreciation. Neither does it preclude the introduction of numerous elective courses at the High School level.

Extra-curricular activities, all enriching character development, need to be varied and complementary to the basic curriculum.

SECTION 3: *TEXTBOOKS*. Textbooks and resource materials should be state controlled and up-dated regularly. The Ministry of Education should approve all textbooks used in public schools.

Article 7 – Finance

SECTION 1: *STATE FUNDING*. Funds for all public schools within a state should be allocated solely by the state government. These funds should be collected by both state and federal governments. Revenue sources will vary from country to country, but they will usually include residential property taxes, commercial property taxes, sales taxes, income taxes, and an education tax.

The principle of encouraging every citizen, regardless of possession or lack of possession of property or belongings, to pay for the education of a nation's children and youth is important in a democratic society. This includes financing the establishment, maintenance, and modernization of all public schools within a state. Revenue sources should include a special education tax, to be used solely for public education.

Federal governments, while not involved in the governance of education within each state, need to collect and allocate funds to education, the primary purpose of which is to ensure equality of education throughout the nation. State governments need to allocate funds to ensure equalization throughout their states, so education in remote regions is comparable to, even though slightly different from, that received in major centres of the state. Allowance must be made for wide variations in local conditions.

No federal, state or local funds should be given to parochial, private, dissentient, denominational, separate, independent or non-governmental schools.

Under no circumstances should school boards, school districts or municipal bodies be permitted to raise funds through local taxation for the operation of their schools, because of the inequity in funding that results from this practice.

SECTION 2: *CONTINGENCY FUND.* Every school district should be given at start-up a contingency fund equal to 10% of its initial operating budget. Monies for this fund shall be deposited in a savings account within the school district, and the initial capital shall not be depleted in any way during the existence of the school district. Monies may be added at any time. The monies earned from the interest may be used by the School Board in any way it wishes.

SECTION 3: *SALARIES AND HONORARIUMS.* Teachers' salaries shall be negotiated on a state basis between a chief negotiator for the state government and a chief negotiator for the state teachers' organization. Both negotiators may include representatives from their respective bodies. Principals and Assistant Principals shall remain members of the teachers' organization while in these administrative positions and shall have representation on the teachers' negotiating body.

Negotiations should begin four months prior to the expiry of each contract. If no agreement is reached within the first eight weeks, a mediator shall be selected from a list of professional mediators acceptable to both chief negotiators. If no agreement is reached by the end of the twelfth week, the items still in dispute shall be referred to a three-member arbitration board, with one arbitrator chosen by the teachers' group, one chosen by the state government and the third member (to serve as chairman) chosen by the two arbitrators. Arbitration shall not be final proposal arbitration, but it shall be binding on both parties and shall be concluded before the expiry of the current contract.

All contracts shall be for at least two years.

Neither lock-outs, strikes nor disruptive actions shall be allowed to interfere with the education of a state's children and youth.

All costs for negotiation, mediation, and arbitration shall be borne by the Ministry of Education.

All salaries, allowances, and working conditions for teachers, school administrators, and support staff are negotiable.

Under no circumstances shall salaries and allowances for school administrators, district administrators (including the Superintendent of Schools and Assistant Superintendents), and support staff be in excess of the maximum salary for teachers within a state.

Each member of a Board of Governors shall be paid an honorarium by the Ministry of Education to cover expenses and provide compensation for time taken from other responsibilities.

Salaries for men and women in all categories shall be identical.

Article 8 – Obligations

SECTION 1: *PREPARATION.* Parents should ensure their children attend school prepared to learn. This includes daily attendance for the full school day, punctuality, and an application to studies and activities. It also includes encouraging compliance with school rules and regulations and standards of conduct, including respect for all and civility in dealings with teachers, administrators, and other students. It also includes carrying out in a reasonable manner all work assigned. Revenge or retaliation should never be permitted in schools, and under no circumstances shall there be any profanity, vulgarity, pornography, drugs, alcohol, vandalism or violence within a school or at a school-run function.

SECTION 2: *PEACE AND ORDER.* It is imperative that all students learn in a peaceful atmosphere. And it is incumbent upon administrators, teachers, and parents to ensure that nothing disrupts that atmosphere. If there is a major disruption, Principals shall be authorized by law to call upon a constable or a peace-keeping officer to restore peace and remove if necessary any individual causing a disturbance.

SECTION 3: *COMPLIANCE.* If a student fails to comply with the school rules, regulations, and standards of conduct, he or she shall be removed from the school.

SECTION 4: *PERFORMANCE.* All students are expected to perform to the best of their ability in every course and activity. Evaluation of performance shall be conducted annually in grades 5, 8, and 12 in the academic areas of the native language, history and geography, mathematics, and science. State examinations shall be conducted annually in all major academic areas in the graduating year.

SECTION 5: *REPORTING TO PARENTS.* All student progress reports shall be in the form of comments for the entire Primary School years. Reports for the Middle School and High School years shall be in the form of letter grades and comments. Wherever possible comments should indicate development along moral, mental, emotional, social, physical, creative, and spiritual lines.

Article 9 – Transportation and Housing

SECTION 1: *ACCOMMODATION*. In isolated or remote regions of a state accommodation for all teachers and administrators shall be provided at a reasonable rate. Full costs of maintenance of the accommodation shall be borne by the Ministry of Education.

SECTION 2: *TRANSPORTATION*. Transportation shall be provided by district School Boards for all students living beyond four kilometres from their neighbourhood school. In certain cases this may be in the form of reimbursement for travel costs.

A school bus of appropriate size should be stationed permanently at every remote or isolated school having access to a road or roads that lead to larger cultural centres. This bus should be for the sole use of the school and should not be used by other community groups. Only fully licensed bus drivers shall operate such a bus. Safety checks of every school bus must be made every month of operation.

Article 10 – Buildings and Grounds

SECTION 1: *SCHOOL BUILDINGS*. The Minister of Education for every state shall have in place a plan for the construction, renewal, and replacement of all schools within the state. It shall include plans for the modernization and replacement of structures every fifty to sixty years. All buildings must be kept abreast of the times and attractive in design and construction. They must also be practical and functional, and be able to incorporate the latest in technology. Students, teachers, and administrators must be kept on the cutting edge of human progress. Keeping buildings up to date is part of that progress.

SECTION 2: *SCHOOL SITES.* The Board of Governors for every school district must secure well in advance sites for the construction and replacement of all schools within their jurisdiction, including an abundance of outdoor playing surface. Expropriation of surrounding properties and buildings may have to be undertaken to guarantee this abundance. Appropriate replacement property and buildings shall be found for those owning expropriated property and buildings. All sites must be attractively landscaped.

SECTION 3: *BUILDING AND SITE COORDINATION.* The Minister of Education shall maintain a central department dealing solely with school buildings and sites throughout a state. This department shall be responsible, through the Minister of Education, for the coordination of expropriation, construction, renewal, and funding for all school capital projects. A master plan of all buildings and sites and plans for their renewal shall be maintained by this department.

All capital projects shall be financed by the Ministry of Education.

This legislative guide provides direction for establishment of the laws, rules, and regulations necessary for maintaining the beauty and effectiveness of public education throughout the world.

APPENDIX A

A Philosophy of Public Education

All education is the elevation of character. For character to be elevated or unfolded children and young people need to grow morally, mentally, emotionally, socially, physically, creatively, and spiritually.

Here spiritual refers to love of good in any form with emphasis on love of one another; moral refers to an awareness of right and wrong and a willingness to act in accord with what is nearest right; mental refers to cultivation of things of the mind and an ability to think for oneself; emotional refers to expression and control of feelings, sensitivity to the feelings of others, and a consideration of those feelings; social refers to the ability and willingness to interact with others on a wholesome basis; physical refers to participation in vigorous physical activities; and creative refers to cultivation of an attitude that promotes fresh approaches to problems and their solutions.

Development in all these areas occurs gradually as students of diverse religions, races, philosophies, and ways of life move together through a carefully designed curriculum. Prime responsibility for this development rests with the home and is assisted by the school's focus on individual growth through all these dimensions.

The results after 12 or 13 years of conscientious instruction by teachers of high moral standards should be an educated citizen – thoughtful, respectful, cooperative, and principled; an independent thinker, a problem-solver, a producer, an individual of action dedicated to making a constructive contribution to the world in any areas of choice.

APPENDIX B

Ten Essentials of Successful Public Education

1   A philosophy based on the premise that all education is the development of character

2   High standards of conduct and performance for teachers and students

3   One basic curriculum

4   Teacher autonomy in methods of instruction

5   No political or religious interference

6   Supportive parental involvement

7   Rotation in administration

8   Equality of funding

9   Appointed boards of governors

10 High ethical or moral standards

𝒥ndex